This well-being journal belongs to

_____

My year of dwelling well begins on

_____

Surely your goodness and love will follow me all the days of my life, and I will dwell in the house of the LORD forever.

PSALM 23:6

Cover design by Nicole Dougherty

Cover photos © Essem Creatives / Creative Market; vodoleyka, Beautiful_textures / Getty Images

Dwelling Well

Copyright © 2020 by Melissa Michaels
Published by Harvest House Publishers
Eugene, Oregon 97408
www.harvesthousepublishers.com

ISBN 978-0-7369-7967-2 (pbk)

Printed in China

19 20 21 22 23 24 25 26 27 / RDS-AR / 10 9 8 7 6 5 4 3 2 1

dwelling well

MELISSA MICHAELS

HARVEST HOUSE PUBLISHERS
EUGENE, OREGON

Dear Friend,

Whether you are a journal lover or someone who buys planners more for decor than to map your days, I believe you're holding this guide in your hands for a reason! I hope it inspires you to intentionally create healthy changes and live a life you love.

In my book *Dwelling*, I explore how our two dwellings—home and body—are interdependent. When we nurture one, we support the other. When we honor both, we change our lives. This begins when we identify and develop healthy habits that serve us as individuals. And it's accomplished through intentional baby steps, one day at a time, one month at a time, one year at a time (rinse and repeat), leading us to a new path...and it's a great one. I promise.

Without intending to, many of us delay prioritizing our well-being for a future season of life—an action that compounds the difficulties we currently struggle with. Good news! You can begin your journey right now. Your year of dwelling well starts today, no matter what day it is. No more putting off the life you long to experience.

This journal is simple, flexible, and personal. The guided pages will help you stay focused on realistic action steps and mind-set shifts no matter how challenging your days become. And even though this journal *is* pretty, it's made for more than decor. You'll look forward to how much better you feel when you use it.

If you have a copy of *Dwelling*, you can use the journal to complement your reading, although the book isn't required. This journal is its own unique, transforming experience.

We'll start with "Goals for My Year of Dwelling Well" followed by an easy-reference guide to the monthly helps so you can dive into your first month with joy and purpose. Use these pages *well*. The positivity you dwell on will overflow into real change in your home, body, and soul. It will inspire you to live a different story this year—the story I know you are ready to create.

BE WELL,
Melissa

---

*This is the beginning of
living a more intentional,
full, whole, and happy life.*

GOALS FOR MY YEAR OF DWELLING WELL

Make this a year to do immeasurable good for your health, your home, and others! The Healthy Goals planning pages set you on a trajectory toward positive change and give you a place to reflect back on each month. How can you nurture your body, turn your home into a sanctuary, and reach out to others this year?

Healthy Body Goals

New habits I want to form:
Example: *Include cardio and strength exercise each week.*

Unhealthy habits to quit:
Example: *Late-night snacking and screen time.*

I will practice self-care by:
Example: *Replacing negative self-talk with nourishing words.*

Healthy Home Goals

How I want my home to feel:
Example: *Clean, intentional, and inviting.*

Spaces I want to refresh:
Example: *Master bedroom to inspire better rest.*

Traditions I want to start:
Example: *Sharing grace and gratitude when at the dining table.*

Healthy Connection Goals

Who I want to connect with this year:
Example: *Extended family and a friend I miss.*

Specific ways I will extend kindness:
Example: *Grocery shop with my elderly neighbor.*

Joyful reasons to open my home and life to community:
Example: *I will celebrate seasons and friends by hosting our couples' group this spring.*

HEALTHY BODY GOALS

New habits I want to form:

_____

_____

_____

Unhealthy habits to quit:

_____

_____

_____

I will practice self-care by:

_____

_____

_____

*If we learn to pay attention to even the
smallest details of how we live, we'll
discover endless opportunities to better
nourish ourselves and the people we love.*

HEALTHY HOME GOALS

How I want my home to feel:

_____

_____

_____

Spaces I want to refresh:

_____

_____

_____

Traditions I want to start:

_____

_____

_____

Each person has a unique story of how their journey to self-care began.

HEALTHY CONNECTION GOALS

Who I want to connect with this year:

_____

_____

_____

Specific ways I will extend kindness:

_____

_____

_____

Joyful reasons to open my home and life to community:

_____

_____

_____

*Prioritizing time and energy to build
community and develop healthy relationships
can make a big difference in our life.*

MONTHLY DWELL WELL HELPS

Every month, these simple offerings invite you to set intentions, be mindful of your choices and goals, and journal to recognize and celebrate all that nurtures your home, body, and soul.

Mindful Wellness Planner

At the beginning of every month, set a self-care appointment to fill out this portion. This is your space to plan your month of wellness intentions and encourage yourself with a personal message.

Self-Care Intention: What actions or decisions will help you care for your body, mind, and spirit?

Example: *Read a Bible verse every night before bed. Exercise three times a week.*

Sanctuary Intention: What steps can you take to improve the health, beauty, or comfort of your surroundings?

Example: *Clear out unused items in three closets. Create more white space on surface areas.*

Acts of Kindness Intention: How might you extend encouragement to others?

Example: *Deliver a welcome gift bag to the new neighbors. Choose one friend to pray for daily.*

Letter to Self: Be your best advocate. Kick off the month with a short note to yourself focusing on the well-being you want to experience over the next 30 days.

Example: *Hi, Self! You're ready to make this pursuit of a healthy, whole life a priority. Begin each day ready to experience the joy and satisfaction of positive changes. You've got this!*

My Word of the Month

Choose a monthly inspiration word. For 30 days, this word or motto can be your touchstone when you need motivation. Not sure which word to choose? To spark ideas, every month starts with a quote from my book *Dwelling* and features a short list of inspiration words.

Month-at-a-Glance

The calendar pages are undated so you can start your year of change and joy now—whether it is January or June. Either fill in all the dates as you envision the year or fill in each month as you turn the new calendar page. Track plans and successes with creative icons, stickers, colors, or whatever strikes your fancy! Here are a few creative icon ideas. Feel free to create your own.

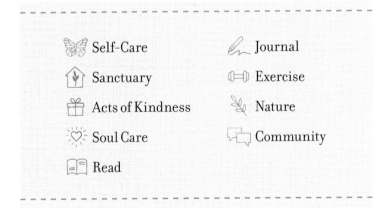

Self-Care

Journal

Sanctuary

Exercise

Acts of Kindness

Nature

Soul Care

Community

Read

Daily Dwellings

Throughout the month, journal your insights, hopes, and experiences related to the Mindful Wellness Planner topics: self-care, sanctuary, and acts of kindness. These pages will keep you focused and transform intentions into action and hope. Here are some prompts to get your own ideas in motion.

Self-Care

- What have you done this month to nurture your body, mind, and soul?
- What most motivates you in areas of rest, exercise, soul care, nutrition, and finding balance?
- Write out verses or quotes you want to meditate on. List prayer requests.

Sanctuary

- Explore the status and progress of your home's health in areas such as cleanliness/clutter, visual appeal, organization and storage solutions, comfort, toxin elimination, and beauty.
- Note inspirations you've seen online, in magazines, or out in the world.
- How have you felt more at home in your own dwelling this month?

Acts of Kindness

- Create a running list of simple ways to inspire kindness.
- When has someone extended kindness to you?
- Grow your gratitude by keeping a record of the acts of kindness you witness daily.

Monthly Journal Invitations

Each month I offer four unique journal prompts and space to write your reflections. These invitations will help you appreciate and enhance your efforts to shape a life that inspires your home, body, and soul.

Savor the Moments

My favorite moment. Every month, turn to this page to honor experiences with gratitude. Reflect on special family moments. When you notice positive changes or someone compliments you, record it to remind yourself what is true. Document the sights, sounds, scents, and feelings experienced during a nature walk. Savor life!

INSPIRATION FOR HEALTHY ROUTINES

Routines create momentum to carry you forward. Choose one for the morning and the evening to support you and your goals. Here are a few possibilities.

Morning : Go for a walk. Sit in silence to savor your coffee. Memorize a verse or a special quote. Make a list of your self-care, sanctuary, and acts of kindness hopes for the day. Respond to a journal invitation from this book. Do stretches to inspiring music. Call someone just to say hi. Review your goals and calendar.

Evening : Set a technology curfew for yourself. Read a book. Take a bath. Spend time in prayer. Listen to relaxing music. Recall a verse or quote from the morning. Run the dishwasher and set the table for breakfast to give you a head start tomorrow. Write an entry in a gratitude journal.

We can design the whole of our lives to be more beautiful & balanced.

Mindful Wellness Planner

for the Month of

_____

Self-Care Intention: _____

_____

_____

Sanctuary Intention: _____

_____

_____

Acts of Kindness Intention: _____

_____

_____

Letter to Self: _____

_____

_____

_____

_____

_____

Word of the Month

_____

Beginnings • Balance • Design • Dream
Wholeness • Confidence • Motivation

MONTH OF

monday	tuesday	wednesday	thursday

MY WORD OF THE MONTH

friday	saturday	sunday	notes

<u>Mar 4 '20</u>

The Sand Village — Balsa Puerto
                    chute to pond water

Sachavaca — Valenancia (Norma's moms)
   — V. had 11 children — some died —
   — newer village — near Libertad
~~Bel~~ Nueva Vida — where we spent the
   most time — then downriver to Libertad —
houses on both sides of airstrips —
church every evening, even when we
weren't there, because most of the
adults didn't read —
We always flew out to N.V.

Balance brings peace.

Bellavista — walked to it thru the jungle, from the sand village (Balsa Puerto)

- Rivers: Sillay (Sachavaca)
      Parañapura (Nueva Vida)
   (tributaries of the Marañon) -
1st village we went to — Soledad
      (Coco's village — (Violeta)
not many believers —

Each summer — we went to about half of the villages — Harts went to the others —

DAILY DWELLINGS
Acts of Kindness

Invite a friend on the wellness journey.

JOURNAL INVITATION #1

How would you describe a healthy, joy-giving home?

JOURNAL INVITATION #2

What motivates you to become your most confident self this year?

JOURNAL INVITATION #3

Write down seven healthy self-care activities you can treat yourself to this month (soothing bath, healthy home-cooked meal, evening tea, coloring in a coloring book, journaling, nature walk, therapeutic cleaning frenzy, creating a happy playlist, and so on). Add them to your self-care intentions in this month's Mindful Wellness Planner.

JOURNAL INVITATION #4

Dream building time. Set aside 30 to 45 minutes to write out dreams for your future. Describe your very best life. How would you spend your time and money if you could? Don't write out your limitations or the "why nots." Instead, explore the "what ifs"!

Savor the Moments

The journey
to "dwell well"
will reveal
gifts of new
possibilities.

Mindful Wellness Planner
for the Month of

_____

Self-Care Intention:

_____

_____

Sanctuary Intention:

_____

_____

Acts of Kindness Intention:

_____

_____

Letter to Self:

_____

_____

_____

_____

Word of the Month

_____

Journey • Health • Presence • Create
Notice • Discover • Possibility

MONTH OF

monday	tuesday	wednesday	thursday
☐	☐	☐	☐
☐	☐	☐	☐
☐	☐	☐	☐
☐	☐	☐	☐
☐	☐	☐	☐
☐	☐	☐	☐

friday	saturday	sunday	notes

DAILY DWELLINGS

Self-Care

You can lean into faith for renewal.

Sanctuary

Notice what delights you in your home.

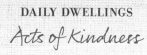

DAILY DWELLINGS

Acts of Kindness

A generous person will prosper; whoever refreshes others will be refreshed. —Proverbs 11:25

JOURNAL INVITATION #1

Describe your current state of health—mind, body, and soul.
In what ways could you improve in those areas this year?

There is a correlation between what is in your home and how you feel! Where in your home are opportunities to make improvements? (For example, home decor, clutter, toxic household products, and so on.)

List five ways you could treat your home as a gift to yourself and others.

What are your spiritual values? In what way is your
faith reflected in your daily habits?

Savor the Moments

Health's, happiness, joy, and a sense of well-being come from good daily habits & wise daily choices.

Mindful Wellness Planner
for the Month of

_____

Self-Care Intention:

_____

_____

Sanctuary Intention:

_____

_____

Acts of Kindness Intention:

_____

_____

Letter to Self:

_____

_____

_____

_____

Word of the Month

_____

Wisdom • Commitment • Baby Steps
Purpose • Gladness • Wellness • Progress

monday	tuesday	wednesday	thursday

MY WORD OF THE MONTH

friday	saturday	sunday	notes

Exhale excuses and breathe in possibilities.

Sanctuary

Your home is a shelter for body, mind, and soul.

Friendship inspires fellowship and self-discovery.

JOURNAL INVITATION #1

Write down your fitness routine and how you feel as a result. If you don't have one, what would be one step you could take to get started?

JOURNAL INVITATION #2

What is something you've always wanted to try or do?
What holds you back? How could you take action to make it happen?

JOURNAL INVITATION #3

What is your favorite room in your home and why?
How does that room make you feel?

JOURNAL INVITATION #4

What activities inspire you? What did you used to love doing with your time? How could you incorporate them into your life more often?

Savor the Moments

Transforming our home
into a sanctuary where
health and restoration are
valued and healthy
relationships are built
transforms _us_.

Mindful Wellness Planner
for the Month of

_____

Self-Care Intention: _____

_____

Sanctuary Intention: _____

_____

Acts of Kindness Intention: _____

_____

Letter to Self: _____

_____

_____

_____

_____

Word of the Month

_____

*Refuge • Becoming • Priorities • Grace
Restoration • Transformation • Treasured*

MONTH OF

monday	tuesday	wednesday	thursday

MY WORD OF THE MONTH

friday	saturday	sunday	notes

DAILY DWELLINGS
Self-Care

_____

_____

_____

_____

_____

_____

_____

_____

_____

_____

_____

_____

_____

_____

_____

_____

*Because of the Lord's great love we are not consumed, for
his compassions never fail. They are new every morning;
great is your faithfulness.* —Lamentations 3:22-23

DAILY DWELLINGS

Sanctuary

Make room for what you love.

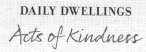

_____

_____

_____

_____

_____

_____

_____

_____

_____

_____

_____

_____

_____

_____

_____

_____

Hospitality opens your home and your heart.

What are three homemaking habits you want to improve on? How?

JOURNAL INVITATION #2

What difficulty are you going through right now that could be viewed as a gift in some way? How can you transform your perspective about a trial or obstacle?

Your home should be your refuge—a safe place to land. Contemplate the ways you could reflect that mind-set in your home.

JOURNAL INVITATION #4

How could you adjust your expectations for what you need to
accomplish in a day to give yourself grace and make room for rest?

Savor the Moments

The only way
to find the
fulfillment
we're searching
for is to
fully invest
ourselves in what
is available
to us—the **LIFE**
right in front
of us.

Mindful Wellness Planner
for the Month of

_____

Self-Care Intention: _____

_____

_____

Sanctuary Intention: _____

_____

_____

Acts of Kindness Intention: _____

_____

_____

Letter to Self: _____

_____

_____

_____

_____

Word of the Month

_____

*Gratitude • Invest • Hope • Contentment
Belonging • Fulfilled • Lovely*

MONTH OF

monday	tuesday	wednesday	thursday
☐	☐	☐	☐
☐	☐	☐	☐
☐	☐	☐	☐
☐	☐	☐	☐
☐	☐	☐	☐
☐	☐	☐	☐

MY WORD OF THE MONTH

friday	saturday	sunday	notes

DAILY DWELLINGS
Self-Care

Whatever is true, whatever is noble, whatever is right, whatever is pure, whatever is lovely, whatever is admirable—if anything is excellent or praiseworthy—think about such things. —Philippians 4:8

DAILY DWELLINGS

Sanctuary

Gratitude transforms the space you have.

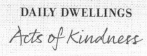

Acts of Kindness

Plan a coffee or tea date with a friend.

JOURNAL INVITATION #1

How does your bedroom invite you to relax and rejuvenate? What are some simple changes or additions you could make that would make this important room feel like your sanctuary?

JOURNAL INVITATION #2

Set a timer for ten minutes and ponder things you
love about yourself. Make a list!

JOURNAL INVITATION #3

Write out ten things you love about your home.

What are tangible habits you can practice to make yourself feel pretty and strong in the morning? (For example, start the day with a walk, wear pink, apply a soothing moisturizer, hydrate with water before you start the coffee, choose a signature scent, put on an outfit that gives you confidence, wear a favorite or meaningful piece of jewelry, and so on.)

Savor the Moments

We can set a mood in our home that nurtures our Mind, Body, and Soul.

Mindful Wellness Planner
for the Month of

_____

Self-Care Intention:

_____

_____

Sanctuary Intention:

_____

_____

Acts of Kindness Intention:

_____

_____

Letter to Self:

_____

_____

_____

_____

_____

Word of the Month

_____

Provision • Savor • Potential • Satisfaction
Intention • Slow Down • Joy

MONTH OF

monday	tuesday	wednesday	thursday
☐	☐	☐	☐
☐	☐	☐	☐
☐	☐	☐	☐
☐	☐	☐	☐
☐	☐	☐	☐
☐	☐	☐	☐

MY WORD OF THE MONTH

friday	saturday	sunday	notes

Self-Care

Give yourself permission to slow down.

Sanctuary

Whoever dwells in the shelter of the Most High will rest in the shadow of the Almighty. I will say of the Lord, "He is my refuge and my fortress, my God, in whom I trust." —Psalm 91:1-2

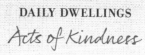

Prayer is an act of compassion and connection.

JOURNAL INVITATION #1

What makes you laugh? Make a list of ways
you could lighten your own mood.

JOURNAL INVITATION #2

Make a list of "feel good" foods. How can you incorporate those into more meals so you and your family are better nourished? Consider starting a food journal to see if you can find a correlation between food and how you feel.

Make a list of people who inspire you to be your best self. How might you spend more time being influenced by these people?

JOURNAL INVITATION #4

Make a season-inspired bucket list of activities that will bring joy to your life and create happy memories for you and the people you love.

Savor the Moments

We can THRIVE best when we kick out the junk, live with greater simplicity, and focus on what serves us well.

Mindful Wellness Planner

for the Month of

_____

Self-Care Intention: _____

_____

_____

Sanctuary Intention: _____

_____

Acts of Kindness Intention: _____

_____

Letter to Self: _____

_____

_____

_____

Word of the Month

_____

Clarity • Ease • Appreciate • Simplify
Courage • Support • Declutter

MONTH OF

monday	tuesday	wednesday	thursday

MY WORD OF THE MONTH

friday	saturday	sunday	notes

Self-Care

Priorities matter. Put first things first.

Sanctuary

Create a place for solitude.

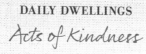

DAILY DWELLINGS

Acts of Kindness

Paring down to an authentic life invites others to be vulnerable.

JOURNAL INVITATION #1

Brainstorm three FREE things you could change in your home that would make you feel more joyful in your surroundings. Make a list below. (Ideas: declutter something, print out free printable inspiring quotes, make something, add a lamp from another room to warm up a dreary space, and so on.)

JOURNAL INVITATION #2

List your basic wellness essentials. What go-to actions and foods does
your body need to function at its best? Which extras are weighing you
down physically or mentally? List ways you want to meet your body's
needs every day.

How could the phrase "don't sweat the small stuff" be incorporated into the atmosphere of your home?

What simple spiritual habits and practices refresh your soul?

Savor the Moments

We don't have to do everything perfectly, but we need to be at peace with our choices.

Mindful Wellness Planner

for the Month of

_____

Self-Care Intention: _____

_____

_____

Sanctuary Intention: _____

_____

_____

Acts of Kindness Intention: _____

_____

_____

Letter to Self: _____

_____

_____

_____

_____

Word of the Month

_____

Positive • Celebrate • Release • Change
Peace • Choice • Streamline

MONTH OF

monday	tuesday	wednesday	thursday
☐	☐	☐	☐
☐	☐	☐	☐
☐	☐	☐	☐
☐	☐	☐	☐
☐	☐	☐	☐
☐	☐	☐	☐

MY WORD OF THE MONTH

friday	saturday	sunday	notes
☐	☐	☐	
☐	☐	☐	
☐	☐	☐	
☐	☐	☐	
☐	☐	☐	
☐	☐	☐	

Contemplate a new way of being.

DAILY DWELLINGS
Sanctuary

An uncluttered home supports a healthy lifestyle.

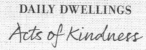

DAILY DWELLINGS
Acts of Kindness

For where your treasure is, there your heart will be also. —Matthew 6:21

JOURNAL INVITATION #1

Do you sit at the table for dinner? Why or why not? What are some new dinnertime traditions you would like to bring into your home?

JOURNAL INVITATION #2

How could you make eating healthy meals more of a savored and cele-
brated experience?

JOURNAL INVITATION #3

Think about how to incorporate more of your senses into your daily home habits (taste, sight, touch, smell, and sound). How could a healthy use of senses create positive associations for you to improve your mood or inspire you to action?

Describe the value of being surrounded by a positive, healthy community. How could you improve in this area? In what ways could you be more intentional with inviting others into your community?

Savor the Moments

Enjoying time in nature is a simple thing you can do for your well-being and self-care.

Mindful Wellness Planner
for the Month of

_____

Self-Care Intention: _____

_____

_____

Sanctuary Intention: _____

_____

_____

Acts of Kindness Intention: _____

_____

_____

Letter to Self: _____

_____

_____

_____

_____

Word of the Month

_____

Adventure • Refreshment • Light • Recreation
Harmony • Inspiration • Freedom

MONTH OF

monday	tuesday	wednesday	thursday
☐	☐	☐	☐
☐	☐	☐	☐
☐	☐	☐	☐
☐	☐	☐	☐
☐	☐	☐	☐
☐	☐	☐	☐

friday	saturday	sunday	notes

DAILY DWELLINGS

Self-Care

Soak up wonder as you wander.

DAILY DWELLINGS

Sanctuary

Welcome color, light, and nature's abundance.

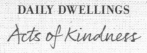

DAILY DWELLINGS
Acts of Kindness

_____

_____

_____

_____

_____

_____

_____

_____

_____

_____

_____

_____

_____

Pluck a flower just for you; gather a bunch and share a few.

JOURNAL INVITATION #1

A good night's sleep is imperative for a healthy mind and body! Write about what helps you have your best night sleep and what keeps you from it. What are some healthy changes you could make to inspire a better night sleep? (For example, calming essential oils, shutting down the computer or TV earlier in the evening, reading a relaxing book before bed, and so on.)

JOURNAL INVITATION #2

What are some ways you could better savor the beauty of life?

JOURNAL INVITATION #3

Journal about how time in nature impacts your mood. When was the last time you took a walk through a forest, park, or beach? Treat yourself to a nature walk and bring back something organic to inspire a calm atmosphere in your home.

JOURNAL INVITATION #4

Describe your life as an adventure where the path you are on
now leads to unexpected and abundant joy. Dream big!

Savor the Moments

You don't
have to
hold your
breath
and hold
up the
world.

Mindful Wellness Planner

for the Month of

_____

Self-Care Intention: _____

_____

_____

Sanctuary Intention: _____

_____

_____

Acts of Kindness Intention: _____

_____

_____

Letter to Self: _____

_____

_____

_____

_____

Word of the Month

_____

Breathe • Nourishment • Energy
Strength • Rejoice • Growth • Healing

monday	tuesday	wednesday	thursday

MY WORD OF THE MONTH

friday	saturday	sunday	notes

Nourish the hope inside of you.

Your home serves a daily visual feast.

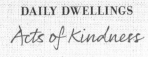

A table set with an extra place is a beautiful sight.

JOURNAL INVITATION #1

How could you make the mood of your home feel
less serious and more lighthearted?

_____

_____

_____

_____

_____

_____

_____

_____

_____

_____

_____

_____

_____

_____

JOURNAL INVITATION #2

List activities that would make you feel more energized and alive.

JOURNAL INVITATION #3

How does your home tell your story? What mementos could you
invite in to make your home reflect more happy memories?

JOURNAL INVITATION #4

List ten ways you want to add beauty to ordinary days.

Savor the Moments

The
connections
we invest in
can change
the course of
our life and
the lives
around us.

Mindful Wellness Planner
for the Month of

_____

Self-Care Intention: _____

_____

_____

Sanctuary Intention: _____

_____

_____

Acts of Kindness Intention: _____

_____

_____

Letter to Self: _____

_____

_____

_____

_____

Word of the Month
_____

Share • Gather • Community
Vulnerability • Belong • Acceptance • Love

MONTH OF

monday	tuesday	wednesday	thursday

MY WORD OF THE MONTH

friday	saturday	sunday	notes

DAILY DWELLINGS
Self-Care

You belong.

As for me and my house, we will serve the LORD. —Joshua 24:15 NASB

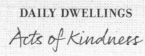

Breaking bread with another will feed your soul.

JOURNAL INVITATION #1

What are seasonal traditions you love? What feels like an obligation or doesn't bring joy to your life? What new traditions would you enjoy and how could you incorporate them into the season?

JOURNAL INVITATION #2

Write down how you feel when you walk in your front door. What would make coming home a more calming ritual? What would make your house feel more cheerful and welcoming?

What are some tangible ways you could help people in need? Think about things you take for granted that you could provide for someone else. Make a list of ways you could meet needs and add action steps to your Mindful Wellness Planner page for this month.

JOURNAL INVITATION #4

Think of five blessings in your life right now. Write about them and why are you are grateful for them. Add these blessings to your gratitude list.

Savor the Moments

Finding
our footing
wherever we are,
with a hopeful
vision for where
we're headed,
is a part
of our journey
to well-
being.

Mindful Wellness Planner

for the Month of

_____

Self-Care Intention:

_____

_____

Sanctuary Intention:

_____

_____

Acts of Kindness Intention:

_____

_____

Letter to Self:

_____

_____

_____

_____

Word of the Month

_____

*Vision • Direction • Thrive • Journey
Momentum • Believe • Faithfulness*

MONTH OF

monday	tuesday	wednesday	thursday
☐	☐	☐	☐
☐	☐	☐	☐
☐	☐	☐	☐
☐	☐	☐	☐
☐	☐	☐	☐
☐	☐	☐	☐

MY WORD OF THE MONTH

friday	saturday	sunday	notes

Celebrate your big and small changes toward health and happiness.

DAILY DWELLINGS

Sanctuary

Make room in your home for unexpected blessings.

Reaching out expands life and hope.

JOURNAL INVITATION #1

What makes your home and life feel sacred?
Which aspects of your relationships feel holy and meaningful?

JOURNAL INVITATION #2

What has surprised you about this year? How have you surprised
yourself? Choose one word that summarizes this year.

JOURNAL INVITATION #3

Why are you glad you dared to pursue this journey
of a healthy home, body, and life?

Write about one healthy home goal, one healthy body goal, and one healthy connection goal you are excited to embrace in your next year of dwelling well.

Savor the Moments

Each season is a
new opportunity
to grow in
our potential,
to be well in all
areas of our life,
to transform
us from the
inside out.

About the Author

Melissa Michaels is a *New York Times* bestselling author and creator of *The Inspired Room*, an award-winning blog that has been one of the top home decorating destinations on the web for more than 11 years. She lives in Seattle with her husband, Jerry; their teen son, Luke; and their adorable doodle pups Jack and Lily. The Michaels' two grown daughters, Kylee and Courtney, are a key part of the creative team at *The Inspired Room*.

You can connect with Melissa and find her blog, social medial channels, and community at **theinspiredroom.net/community**.

Visit **DwellingBook.com** for related resources, downloadable images, and more.

Feel Well Where You Dwell

Our dwellings—both our home and body—are intricately connected. Each has the potential to inspire the other to be its very best!

Your home is where your life happens. Create a sanctuary that inspires your well-being so you can experience greater peace, comfort, and belonging.

Your body, mind, and soul need daily nourishment to help you feel healthy and happy. Discover simple ways to make self-care a priority.

Dwelling will help you

- learn to better care for your home environment so it takes care of you

- make decisions that simplify your life

- create more peace in your day

- invest in relationships that make you feel positive, challenged, and supported

- lean into faith for strength and renewal

Melissa Michaels wants to show you how to live a life that nurtures both your home and body. By making a series of small, intentional choices—from what you bring into your home to how you shape your daily habits and mind-sets—you'll be on your way to a more balanced and happy life!